Greening
Your Church

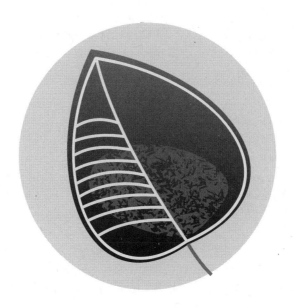

Greening
Your Church

························•························

NORMAN LÉVESQUE

A Practical Guide to Creation Care Ministry
for Parishes, Dioceses and Religious Communities

Foreword by James Weisgerber,
Archbishop emeritus of Winnipeg

NOVALIS

© 2014 Novalis Publishing Inc.

Cover design: Audrey Wells
Cover photograph: Jupiter Images
Layout: Interscript

Published by Novalis

Publishing Office
10 Lower Spadina Avenue, Suite 400
Toronto, Ontario, Canada
M5V 2Z2

Head Office
4475 Frontenac Street
Montréal, Québec, Canada
H2H 2S2

www.novalis.ca

Cataloguing in Publication is available from Library and Archives Canada

Printed in Canada.

The Scripture quotations contained herein are from the New Revised Standard
Version of the Bible, copyrighted 1989 by the Division of Christian Education of
the National Council of the Churches of Christ in the United States of America,
and are used by permission. All rights reserved.

We acknowledge the financial support of the Government of Canada through
the Canada Book Fund for business development activities.

5   4   3   2   1   18   17   16   15   14

*I dedicate this guide to God, our Creator,
because all his works were made in wisdom
and the earth is full of his creatures (Psalm 104:24).*

*I also dedicate it to the one who so encouraged me
to remain true to this mission, the one I love
with all my heart, my spouse, Marie-Audrey.*

*Finally, I wish to thank the many priests and pastoral
workers whose comments, so graciously shared,
enriched the quality of this work. Special thanks to
Bernice and Belva for their help with the translation.*

CONTENTS

FOREWORD

Karl Barth, one of the most prominent theologians of the twentieth century, famously said that a Christian should face the world with the Bible in one hand and the newspaper in the other. Our faith tells us that God has spoken, and God's Word recorded in the Scriptures can be trusted. God actively continues his providential care in the unfolding of history. New realities give us a deeper insight into and understanding of our tradition, and our revealed tradition helps us understand the changing world around us. Scripture help us to understand history, and history helps us to understand Scripture.

The leadership of our churches is calling eloquently and urgently for us to remember that we are stewards of God's good Creation. To be human is to be responsible for tending the great garden that is the earth. Science and technology have given us a much greater understanding of the richness and interconnectedness of all Creation and have discovered myriad ways of altering and exploiting this richness. The best of science is now warning us that our actions and lifestyles are putting the Earth, our home, in serious jeopardy.

The Church's great challenge is to determine how to introduce this urgent message into the imaginations and consciences of the disciples of Jesus. We simply cannot expect our political leaders to resolve these serious issues without our input. People change the minds of politicians, and not the other way around! Our challenge is to get care for the earth, responsibility for Creation, and the threat posed by climate change onto the agendas of parishes, congregations and individual Christians. Stewardship of Creation is a biblical imperative!

To help us in this endeavour, we need practical, user-friendly programs that will empower ordinary people to understand the dangers we face and discover ways to change our practices and lifestyles to mirror our desire to be a biblical people.

Norman Lévesque's book, *Greening Your Church: A Practical Guide to Creation Care and Ministry for Parishes, Dioceses and Religious Communities*, provides the Church with a very useful tool as we allow the present dangerous threats to Creation to help us reread the Bible and understand in new ways that our vocation is to be stewards of the garden. The challenge is great, but God's power and love are greater. We are called to be not only a people of hope, but also a people of action. This book can be a powerful resource as we answer God's call.

+ James Weisgerber

Archbishop emeritus of Winnipeg

PREFACE

A friend once told me that all forms of Church teaching (catechesis, papal statements and Sunday homilies, for example) should be offered with a Bible in one hand and a newspaper in the other. All our pastoral work should certainly be done in this way – especially Creation Care ministry.

The current environmental crisis affects the whole world, but there are three main categories of victims: the vulnerable, future generations, and endangered species.

When the environment is neglected, *vulnerable people* are greatly affected, through illness or poverty resulting from pollution and environmental degradation. Low-income families living next to the industrial zone east of Montreal, for example, have no voice to raise against the pollution that engulfs them. They are also more vulnerable to lung disease, living in that environment. In gospel terms, our brothers and sisters are suffering.

An impoverished environment also has an enormous impact on *future generations*. The United Nations' Intergovernmental Panel on Climate Change outlines a range of consequences of increased global warming for humans: displacement of those living in coastal cities because of rising sea levels, resettlement of refugees who have lost their homes due to more frequent severe storms, health problems among the elderly caused by smog and heat waves, lower water levels in rivers and seaways after glaciers have melted, and reduced harvests and fish catches because of sea warming. In gospel terms, our children will suffer because of our inaction.

Endangered species are another serious issue. Our selfishness is destroying the life that God creates. Careless overexploitation of natural resources often causes irreparable damage to the bio-diversity of ecosystems. When a species is endangered, there are consequences for all the other species with which it interacts. For example, the collapse of the bee population affects pollination and plant fertility in an entire region, which in turn affects harvests. In gospel terms, God's creatures are suffering.

These tragedies are signs of the ecological crisis, which is a result of humanity's disconnection from the rest of Creation. That is why Popes John Paul II, Benedict XVI and Francis have denounced environmental degradation and insisted that the ecological crisis is not primarily a scientific or political crisis, but mainly an ethical one. The words of Saint Paul speak to us today: "We know that the whole creation has been groaning in labour pains until now" (Romans 8:22).

INTRODUCTION

This practical guide for "greening your church" – or Creation Care ministry, as it is more officially called – is designed to equip dioceses, parishes and religious communities not only to praise our Creator, but to really take care of Creation.[1] Ever since Pope Paul VI's speech at the Stockholm Conference in 1972, the Roman Catholic Church has been speaking about the protection of Creation. Numerous Church statements have continued to address this issue over the years. Books on Creation theology are sitting on library shelves, but sadly lacking is guidance on how to integrate Creation Care into pastoral ministry so that our Church can truly fulfill its mandate to "proclaim the good news to the whole creation" (Mark 16:15).

This guide is divided into two main sections:

Part 1, a theological view of Creation, provides an overview of the many treasures relating to the environment that are found in the Christian tradition.

Part 2, a pastoral view of Creation, presents a useful intervention model plus suggested activities that churches can readily undertake.

....

1. Throughout this book, the use of a capital "C" for the word "Creation" acknowledges its sacred origin. This usage signifies "God's Creation" and not simply a human creation, like a painting, a cake or a building.

Creation Care ministry has three main objectives:

1 To cultivate a Christian spirituality that is more closely connected to Creation, inspired by the Bible and the example of the lives of the saints;

2 To raise awareness about one's own environment and about the current suffering of Creation;

3 To reduce the environmental impact of the Christian community by taking care of Creation through the choices we make in our day-to-day actions.

In reading this guide, you will come to realize that environmentalism is not a surface coating applied to the Church, but rather is a faith-based understanding of the ecological crisis facing our planet. You will see in these pages that Christians have already begun to respond to the urgency of this situation with the very best of our tradition: with faith, with hope, with love.

Thanks to your involvement, the Church will no longer merely be towed along wherever the environmental current leads, but will become an active partner in reconciling us with our natural environment and will become the trailblazer of a spirituality that will prepare people for the advent of a "new earth." We are in solidarity with those prophets who warn of what is at stake environmentally, while at the same time taking on our role of instilling hope for a sustainable world.

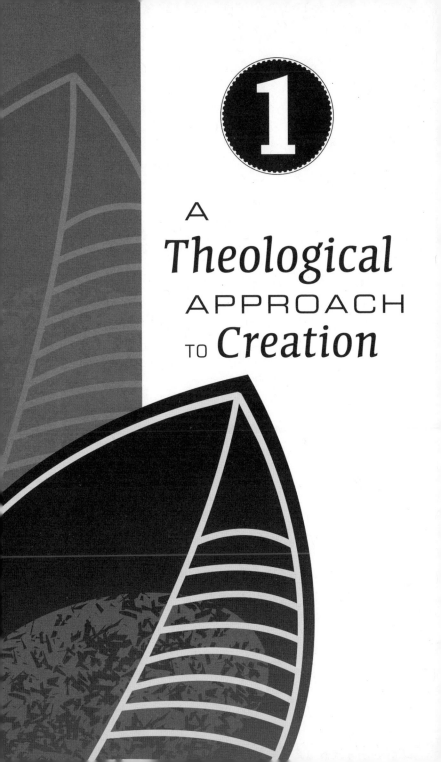

1

A
Theological
APPROACH
TO *Creation*

Pope Benedict XVI challenged the Church to take up a new way of thinking about the environment in his World Day of Peace message of January 1, 2010: "The Church has a responsibility towards creation, and she considers it her duty to exercise that responsibility in public life, in order to protect earth, water and air as gifts of God the Creator meant for everyone." A rich and inspiring theology of Creation lies behind this statement.

A theology of Creation has been rediscovered in recent years by theologians and other inspired Christians. This section presents an overview of what Catholic tradition tells us about the theology of Creation, with special emphasis on the Bible.

Why has the Church's contribution to the environmental movement been so minimal until now?

In fact, the Christian tradition has much to say about our relationship with our environment – this world that God created – as the following pages will prove. This ecological tradition has been largely forgotten, buried under three centuries of Cartesian thought.

In his *Discourse on Method* (1637), Descartes states bluntly that the animal is "a clock composed only of wheels and springs." The "I think, therefore I am" thesis tends to reduce creatures to simple objects, with humans exercising mastery and ownership over nature. The rationalism of Descartes made huge inroads into theology and increased the distance between earth and heaven, body and soul, flesh and spirit. This ideology was taken up by some religious, such as Nicolas Malebranche (1638–1715), a French Oratorian, and Antoine Arnaud (1612–1694), a Jansenist. The disconnect between human beings and their environment is still felt today.

Even before Descartes, we read in the *Sacred Meditations* (1597) of Francis Bacon, "Knowledge is power." The more we know about nature, some people believed, the more power we have over it. This ideology created a deep break with the Christian tradition, which saw knowledge of nature as a way of *gaining* wisdom. Theology was influenced by the utilitarian bent of these ideologies, to the extent that "subdue" the earth (Genesis 1:28) was reinterpreted as permission to exploit nature without restraint. This arrogant mentality led to the deplorable actions during the colonial period, whose painful effects are still felt today.

It is time to rediscover the ecological values that are already present in Christian tradition: biblical accounts, lives of the saints, Eucharistic Prayers, and the virtues.

A new day is dawning for a Christian ecology in which we can rediscover and reappropriate the fullness of our Christian tradition's close communion with nature. In fact, this is a rediscovery of a key aspect of our faith, and it is green because it is filled with new life and hope.

The Theme of the Environment in the Bible

The Old Testament contains a variety of stories that establish a theology of the environment. Our tangible and spiritual relationship with Creation is described in these stories, wise sayings and laws. The New Testament repeats them in a fresh way by adding the figure of Christ, the Word of God through whom all things were made.

The Old Testament

For Catholics, the Old Testament contains 46 books. A number of these books come from various oral traditions dating back more than 3,000 years. They describe the origins and history of the people of Israel in the form of stories that are filled with rich imagery and symbols. These accounts feature such legendary figures as Moses, David and Elijah, who acted as intermediaries between God and the people. The Jewish writers of Antiquity also sought to answer universal and existential questions such as these: What is the meaning of human life? Why are humans on Earth? What is our relationship to animals? What is our relationship to plants? Why was our environment created?

The Old Testament, which we share with the Jewish people, contains the foundation of environmental ethics. It shapes our vision of the world and holds up an inspiring example for our times.

Is the universe just a fluke?

Scientific method, the basis of modern thought, relies on the study of observable phenomena. It is therefore not surprising that scientific research, based on its necessary objectivity, reaches the conclusion that life is the result of random chance. However, this method does not allow for identifying divine action, because divine action is not objectively observable.

On the other hand, the peoples of Antiquity were quick to identify natural phenomena like the sun, the sea and the wind with divinities. The neighbouring peoples to the Israelites – the Egyptians, Greeks and Assyrians – had myths in which the creation of the world was the result of a conflict between the gods. For them, a certain mountain range was the arm of a god, a certain lake was filled with the tears of a goddess, and a certain cave was inhabited by a creature that had been banished by the gods. These ancient peoples often saw the environment as something bad, and they feared it. This pagan way of thinking underwent an astonishing revolution thanks to the Jewish people.

The story of Creation *in seven days* is a different story altogether. The first chapter of the Book of Genesis denounces idolatry of nature and professes faith in one God, who made heaven and earth. It reads like a poem, with the days and nights setting the rhythm. During the first three days, God creates spaces, and during the next three days, God populates these spaces. And at each creative Word, the Earth produces the desired creatures. In God's eyes, no species is evil, bad or detestable. Our environment, filled with a biodiversity created by God, is "very good" (Genesis 1:31). Furthermore, "his compassion is over all that he has made" (Psalm 145:9).

This cry – "It is very good!" – may echo our heart's response to our own experiences of wonder at the sight of a sunset, a valley, a river, a deer. But the tons of concrete in large cities separate us from Creation, and the landscape has been so disfigured, without being restored by those who destroyed it, that the wonder is disappearing and the heart no longer finds it easy to say, "It is very good." If people do not dare drink from a spring or a river, for example, it is no longer "very good." Facing ecological devastation, a new existential question arises: Have we betrayed God's plan?

The author of Proverbs shows that God created everything with wisdom (Proverbs 3:19). A part of this wisdom of Creation is studied by biologists: the balance of ecosystems. The fertility of a living environment is possible only when this balance, meaning the laws of nature, is respected. "The law of the Lord is perfect, reviving the soul" (Psalm 19:7). This concerns all creatures: the survival of human populations is also at stake when the balance is broken. Many of our brothers and sisters throughout the world suffer terribly because the land has become sterile. Decades of intensive agriculture, mainly for export, have ruined the sacred balance of the land.

Where does life come from? What sustains it?

To the best of our current knowledge, we think that life began on Earth some three billion years ago, and then spread, developed and became more complex over the entire surface of the planet – first aquatic animals, then land animals, and finally birds. This sequence of evolution is the result of a competition favouring the fittest creatures, but Creation also evolves through cooperation, symbiosis and mutuality. For example, lichen is the result of symbiosis between a fungus and a microscopic alga. The orchid can be pollinated only by a bee, not by any other insect. Creation, with its countless interactions between creatures, seems to have been lovingly shaped over millions of years. The creative act is not finished; it continues everywhere there is life. According to the Psalmist, life does not generate itself; it is God who gives life: "When you take away their breath, they die and return to their dust. When you send forth your spirit, they are created; and you renew the face of the ground" (Psalm 104:29-30).

God is not only the Creator, but also the Provider. As the Psalmist sings, "These [creatures] all look to you to give them their food in due season; when you give to them, they gather it up; when you open your hand, they are filled with good things" (Psalm 104:27-28). The food chain (herbivores, carnivores, predators, prey) expresses how life is sustained in nature, but we believe that God responds to the needs of all his creatures *through* their environment. Providence is a reality in nature. When we destroy the balance of ecosystems, we are preventing Providence from operating.

In his message of January 1, 2010, Pope Benedict XVI said, "If we care for creation, we realize that God, through creation, cares for us." This passage challenges the modern view of an environment that provides for our needs, emphasizing instead that the environment is a means by which God provides for our needs.

A covenant between God and humanity and with all living creatures

The value God places on biodiversity – the magnificent variety of living beings that coexist with humans – is highlighted in the mythic story of Noah (Genesis 6–9). In the ark, there were two from *each species*! Clearly, each species has a role to play in ecosystems. The rainbow is the sign of the covenant between God, humanity and all creatures. In ecological terms, the creatures are interdependent: we're all in same boat! We can see this as a call to be like Noah and preserve biodiversity.

But humans are superior to other creatures, aren't they?

The current ecological movement goes against the ideology that animals are all "objects" that can be used for our own needs – for instance, a cow is a reserve of milk, the chicken makes a delicious broth, a mouse is a laboratory specimen, a pig gives us bacon, and so on. Often, entire ecosystems are razed in order to build a new shopping mall or residential area without any consideration for the creatures that are living there already. There are no more maples on Maple Street and no more willows in Willowdale. Too often, life is destroyed in the name of profit.

In the face of the system's excesses, ecologists have proposed an egalitarian ethic in which humans and animals have the *same dignity*. Their reaction to abuse is completely understandable, but it must not be forgotten that humankind also has undeniable gifts.

God created humans in his image and gave them intelligence and creativity, rather than leaving them in a "wild" state, which allows them to have dominion over the other animals (Psalm 8). According to the story of Creation, God said to the humans: "Be fruitful and multiply, and fill the earth and subdue it; and have dominion over the fish of the sea and over the birds of the air and over every living thing that moves upon the earth" (Genesis 1:28). But this dominion should be in God's image, the image of a creative and loving God who wants all species to be fruitful.

The humans receive this command to have dominion over Creation in order to give order and promote life, not to destroy everything in their wake. Destroying everything would not make sense. A good comparison would be a teacher who "rules over" the class: she subjects her students to her instructions to help them succeed, not to make them fail. This command is therefore a call to accountability, for humans to be aware of their actions. If you think about it, we cannot have dominion over a clear-cut forest, because nothing remains to have dominion over once we have destroyed it.

What is pollution, according to the Bible?

You will not find the phrase "Protect the environment" in the Bible. Instead, the Bible speaks of a relationship with Creation, rather than reacting to an ecological crisis. However, the prophets denounced the degradation of the environment. Here are two examples:

> How long will the land mourn, and the grass of every field wither? For the wickedness of those who live in it the animals and the birds are swept away. (Jeremiah 12:4)

> The earth lies polluted under its inhabitants; for they have transgressed laws, violated the statutes, broken the everlasting covenant. (Isaiah 24:5)

The prophets of our own day speak out against the harm done to Creation. They see the connections that exist between the current ecological crisis, economic crisis, food crisis and spiritual

crisis. This crisis is the result of a broken covenant, transgressed laws, wickedness and selfishness. If life is put ahead of profit (or comfort), the covenant will be restored.

The Earth belongs to human beings, doesn't it?

Only one passage in the Bible (Psalm 115:16) suggests that God might have bequeathed the Earth to humans so that they become the owners. However, the Bible consistently reminds us that God remains the Lord of the Land, our landlord.

This statement from the Psalmist could not be clearer: "The earth is the Lord's and all that is in it, the world, and those who live in it" (Psalm 24:1). Deuteronomy also points out: "… heaven and the heaven of heavens belong to the Lord your God, the earth with all that is in it …" (Deuteronomy 10:14). And when the people of Israel entered the Promised Land, God reminded them that it did not belong to them: "The land shall not be sold in perpetuity, for the land is mine; with me you are but aliens and tenants" (Leviticus 25:23).

The anthropocentric folly ("human beings come first") of our time, which is at the root of the present ecological crisis, is denounced in the story of Job. Full of himself and his own concerns, he thinks that the universe revolves around our species. But God bombards him with questions that help him rediscover his humility. "Is the wild ox willing to serve you? Will it spend the night at your crib?" (Job 39:9). "Is it at your command that the eagle mounts up and makes its nest on high?" (Job 39:27). The book of Qoheleth (also called Ecclesiastes) requires even more humility from us, since from a biological perspective, humans breathe and die like the other animals: "For the fate of humans and the fate of animals is the same; as one dies, so dies the other. They all have the same breath, and humans have no advantage over the animals; for all is vanity" (Ecclesiastes 3:19).

Humans are therefore not all-powerful, as they often think they are. The moral of the book of Ecclesiastes is that the centre of our world is not humankind, but God. The environmental ethic that emerges from the Bible is not anthropocentric (centred on people), but necessarily theocentric (centred on God). Humans must enter into a relationship with *God's* Creation. It is danger-ous for humanity to act as owner; instead, we must assume our responsibility as steward.

What is the role of humans?

The story of the creation of the first human (Genesis 2) is a won-derful Bible text on the subject of our relationship with Creation. Take a few minutes to reread the second chapter of Genesis.

According to the story, the first human being is a mixture of earth and water, given life by a breath (air). What emerges from these first lines of the Bible, from an ecological reading, is that human beings are intimately related to their environment. The human (*adam*) comes from the earth (*adamah*). Our body is composed of what we eat, drink and breathe. This story reminds us that, in material terms, we are made up of the elements around us. We are terrestrials, not extraterrestrials.

According to this same story, what is the ideal place for the human? We might have imagined a sumptuous palace filled with gold and marble. But no: the earthly paradise is a garden! Home base for the human, from which he is made and where he renews his energy, is in Creation. Many people have told me that they go to nature to truly find themselves. The air is good to breathe.

The ground is soft and welcoming. The trees are pleasant to look at and form beautiful landscapes. The fruit is good to eat. Even the wind blowing through the leaves is melodious.

> The Lord God took the man and put him in the garden of Eden to till it and keep it. (Genesis 2:15)

And what is the human's role in the garden? God invites him to till the soil and keep the garden. The verb meaning *to till* in Hebrew (*lavda*) also means *to serve*. Humans are to serve the earth! Generally, the Bible speaks more often of serving God. But, when you think about it, "serving the earth" and "serving God" will both result in a fruitful life. Also, the concept of service does not apply only to the servant, but also to the master. For instance, parents are constantly serving their children in order to watch them grow, but parents still maintain their authority. Humans have another responsibility: to keep the garden. Keeping means defending it against something. But what? It may well be against our own egotism, which would lead us to take everything from it (including the forbidden fruit).

Here is another key to reading this passage. First, the verb *till* has to do with the idea of developing the land: cutting, sowing, building, arranging. The Brundtland Report (1987) emphasized this positive aspect of development, particularly for poorer countries.[2] Also, the verb *keep* has to do with a long-term vision, a lasting garden. This brings us to the realization that the first few pages of the Bible contain the inspiration for **sustainable development**. The concept is already there, in our Judeo-Christian tradition.

....

2. United Nations, *Report of the World Commission on Environment and Development: Our Common Future* (UN: Geneva, 1987). http://www.un-documents.net/wced-ocf.htm.

Is productivity a virtue?

Productivity is a useful concept, but in our day and age, it has become an obsession and a major cause of environmental degradation. From the construction site to the shopping mall to the factory floor, the ideology of productivity is all-powerful. (Do you remember when stores were closed on Sunday?)

The Bible places great emphasis on the weekly day of rest, the Sabbath. God himself rested and contemplated his work when it was done. The biblical author deduced from this that we should do the same. It is even the fourth commandment: "Observe the sabbath day and keep it holy" (Deuteronomy 5:12-15). The explanation of this commandment is related to being released from slavery in Egypt. Does this suggest that working without ceasing makes us slaves?

The rest commanded by God permits a balanced life. Even the earth is to be allowed to rest every seven years (Leviticus 25:1-7). Productivity is therefore not a biblical virtue; rather, rest, the Sabbath, is the key. When we step off the treadmill, we can meditate, contemplate Creation, be with our Creator. One less day of shopping or work uses fewer resources. It regenerates the Earth, and us as well.

Creation is a holy choir: Praise God with every creature

Music moves the soul. And Creation, when we take the time to contemplate it, has virtually the same effect on us. Does Creation sing? Who does it sing for?

From the opening lines of the Bible, we read that God created everything by his Word. And his creatures, dispersed through time and space, can respond to their Creator. The Bible inspires us to believe that simply by existing, creatures give praise to God. The Psalmist has the creatures sing, one after the other, conducting them like an orchestra:

> Praise the Lord from the earth ...
> mountains and all hills, fruit trees and all cedars!
> Wild animals and all cattle,
> creeping things and flying birds! (Psalm 148:7, 9-10)

The song of three young men in the book of Daniel (3:52-90) is another wonderful example of praise along with all Creation. Our Church would benefit greatly from introducing people to contemplation, to listening to the song of Creation, which would be all the more meaningful in this time of ecological crisis.

The New Testament

The New Testament contains 27 books: the four Gospels, the Acts of the Apostles, the various letters (also called epistles) from Saint Paul and other writers, and the Book of Revelation. These books were written over a fairly short time, roughly between 50 and 100 years after Jesus Christ. They mainly tell of Jesus' ministry and the Good News of God's love that he shared with people during a difficult period of history for the Jews, who were forced to live under the authority of the Roman Empire. The people's concerns were political and social. Humans therefore had a central place in the New Testament writings, and people's relation to Creation was secondary. However, the evangelists and the writers of the letters base their writings on the Old Testament vision of the world, while at the same time integrating Christian hope.

Who created the Earth and who sustains life?

The first chapter of John's Gospel echoes the first chapter of Genesis: "In the beginning was the Word ..." (John 1:1). In looking at the life of Jesus, John the evangelist concludes that the creative Word from the beginning of time, which he had been told about since his youth, was incarnated in Jesus. When God spoke to create, it was Christ himself who created.

In his letter to the Colossians, the Apostle Paul also places Christ at the centre of Creation, "for in him all things in heaven and on earth were created ... all things have been created through him and for him. He himself is before all things, and in him all things hold together" (Colossians 1:16-17).

Because we are heirs to Christian spirituality, we can no longer see the maple tree, the beaver, the frog, the lark and the wolf in the same way. These creatures are in Christ and their lives are held together by him. Destroying vast areas containing living creatures held together by Christ is irresponsible and almost blasphemous. Our faith in Christ inspires us to share space with creatures, because they were created by him and for him.

If Saint Paul's assertion is not surprising enough, then his next statement will certainly give you pause. The Hymn to Christ in the letter to the Colossians ends with these words:

> For in him all the fullness of God was pleased to dwell, and through him God was pleased to reconcile to himself all things, whether on earth or in heaven, by making peace through the blood of his cross. (Colossians 1:19-20)

Jesus the Christ gave himself in love and died on the cross, not just for the salvation of every human being, but to save all of Creation. His saving act ripples through history like a stone cast into a lake, and reaches all the way to us. He is Saviour of all Creation.

What was Jesus' relationship with nature?

After years of manual labour as a carpenter, Jesus meets John the Baptist. Jesus' life is transformed and the Spirit drives him into the wilderness. "He was in the wilderness for forty days ... he was with the wild beasts; and the angels waited on him" (Mark 1:13). Jesus was with the animals, just like Adam was. Jesus thereby inaugurates *paradise regained*, as proclaimed by the prophet Isaiah, where all creatures live in peace (Isaiah 11:6-8). Indeed, the Good News of Jesus Christ is not reserved only for human beings, because Jesus says to his disciples:

66 Go into all the world and proclaim the good news to the whole creation. (Mark 16:15) 99

If we look at the text in the Vulgate (the Latin version of the Bible that Saint Jerome translated in the fourth century), the word *creaturae* means *creatures*, which has an impact on our faith. If we believe that Jesus died to save the whole Creation, it makes sense to consider that we can proclaim the good news to the whole Creation (through our words, but above all through our actions).

While our reflex as modern Christians may be to go and pray in a church or chapel, it was different for Jesus. In reading any of the four Gospels, we are struck by the back-and-forth movement in his life, between his ministry to the crowds and his times of quiet withdrawal to pray in nature: "... he went out to the mountain to pray" (Luke 6:12). In Jesus, there is a balance between contemplation and action.

Jesus also seems to show love for all creatures, even the littlest ones. He therefore teaches that his Father cares for the sparrows; he sees them fall to the ground, even if they do not have much value for us (Matthew 10:29).

Jesus knew the Scriptures well, and he had learned that nature was created with wisdom (see Proverbs 3 and Sirach 17). Furthermore, he was a "country boy" from Nazareth, attuned to the cycle of the seasons, to sowing and reaping, to the vineyards, to shepherding. The list of parables involving nature is a long one: the vine, the sheep, the fig tree, the sower, the setting sun, the tares, the mustard seed, the leaven, the tree and its fruits, and more.

We must admit that priests and pastoral workers do not usually base their teaching on nature. And yet Jesus did it all the time. He recognized that God's wisdom could be found in his Creation. This is something we must discover: the more familiar we are with nature, the more it teaches us spiritual realities (see Job 12:7-8).

When we are consumed with worry, Jesus urges us to look to nature for reassurance. He reminds us how God, our Father, cares for the needs of all his creatures: "Look at the birds of the air; they neither sow nor reap nor gather into barns, and yet your heavenly Father feeds them" (Matthew 6:26). Obviously, if they do not have food, it is because the balance in the ecosystem has been upset. God cannot provide for the birds, or for humans, if we destroy the Creation through which God cares for us.

What should be our relationship to money and wealth?

We need to consume resources to survive, but overconsumption is one of the main causes of degradation of the resources God provides for all creatures. When the economy is put before the environment, the damage can be irreparable. What would Jesus have said about the amount of food wasted, parts that are programmed to break down, and disposable products? These habits are foreign to the kind of austerity Jesus lived: "Foxes have holes, and birds of the air have nests; but the Son of Man has nowhere to lay his head" (Luke 9:58).

The best example of Jesus' opinion of wealth is in his encounter with the rich young man. When Jesus tells him, "... go, sell your possessions ... then come, follow me" (Matthew 19:21), the young man goes away, for he had many possessions. Jesus then makes this famous statement to the others: "Again I tell you, it is easier for a camel to go through the eye of a needle than for someone who is rich to enter the kingdom of God" (Matthew 19:24). Being attached to possessions and trying to manage them causes even more harm today, because it places enormous pressure on natural resources. Jesus adds this powerful phrase: "No slave can serve two masters; for a slave will either hate the one and love the other, or be devoted to the one and despise the other. You cannot serve God and wealth" (Luke 16:13).

In light of the environmental crisis, is there any hope?

Nature gives us signs to interpret. A kayaker can read a river, a mountain climber can read a mountain, a meteorologist can read the sky. Men and women of God, following Jesus' example, also have a special gift for "interpret[ing] the present time" (Luke 12:56).

Saint Paul gives a very particular interpretation of the sufferings of nature. The following passage, while enigmatic, offers hope to all who are affected by the present environmental crisis.

> For the creation waits with eager longing for the revealing of the children of God; for the creation was subjected to futility, not of its own will but by the will of the one who subjected it, in hope that the creation itself will be set free from its bondage to decay and will obtain the freedom of the glory of the children of God. We know that the whole creation has been groaning in labour pains until now. (Romans 8:19-22)

Christians, ecologists and humanity in general dream of a better world. The most inspired of them hope to be agents of change. Indeed, Paul says that we work with Christ to bring this good work to completion (Philippians 1:6). One of the aspects of the new kingdom on Earth, under the reign of God, will be the integrity of Creation.

And so, like Christ, our deepest desire will be to focus not on heaven, but on the Earth! At the end of the story of Christ's return, there is a new Earth, so beautiful and harmonious that it will be almost unrecognizable compared to the old one: "Then I saw a new heaven and a new earth ... And I saw the holy city, the new Jerusalem, coming down out of heaven from God ..." (Revelation 21:1-2). "Then the angel showed me the river of the water of life, bright as crystal, flowing from the throne of God and of the Lamb ..." (Revelation 22:1). Any passage from Revelation must be considered symbolically; it would be naive to think that a city without pollution would literally come down out of heaven. But it remains true that this story gives us Christian hope for the Earth for generations to come.

A warning: Adore the Creator, not his creatures

In spite of the rise of the environmental movement in the 1970s, the Church opposed the philosophy of certain environmentalists. "Tree-hugging" was likened to paganism, because it seemed to be a form of worshipping nature. The divinization of Gaia, the Earth goddess, does not mesh with our theology of one God. Others compare nature to the body of God, a form of pantheism that denies God's transcendence. These spiritualities cannot be reconciled with Christian theology, but to enter into dialogue with people who are seeking spirituality, let us acknowledge that these views can lead to illuminating inspirations for Christians.

The theology of Creation is far from being paganism or pantheism, because worship is directed towards God, not towards creatures. In denouncing the pagan religion of the Greeks and Romans, Saint Paul says that they "exchanged the truth about God for a lie and worshipped and served the creature rather than the Creator, who is blessed forever!" (Romans 1:25).

A pastoral theology of Creation looks in contemplation at Creation, because nature reveals traces of God's glory. Saint Paul affirms that God's qualities can be seen through the things God has made (Romans 1:20). Just as we come to recognize an artist by studying his works, so getting to know Creation can help us to better know the Creator. Enjoy your moments of contemplation!

Ecological Saints

Saint Francis of Assisi

Saint Francis of Assisi's (ca. 1181–1226) biography[3] contains many colourful legends, called *fioretti*. Although they are not always historically factual, they tell us a lot about this holy man of Assisi and point to a Christian environmental ethic.

He was baptized John (Giovanni), and was the son of a wealthy cloth merchant in the village of Assisi, which sits on a hillside in the Umbria region of central Italy. Having made a trip to France, he was nicknamed Francis (Francesco). Living in the Middle Ages, he wanted to become a knight to fight against other kingdoms of Italy, but he fell ill before the first battle, and his life suddenly changed.

Wandering aimlessly about the city, he noticed the suffering of the poor and gave them coats, which made his father angry. The Bishop of Assisi presided over a court where Francis was accused by his father. Francis stripped off all his clothes and threw the bundle of clothing and jewellery at his father, saying, "Now I can truly say 'Our Father who art in heaven.'"

He left the city, completely naked, and was given something to wear by a farmer who took pity on him. He set to work repairing churches, beginning with San Damiano, and then the little Santa Maria degli Angeli. He did the repairs with his own hands, stone by stone. He sang and danced in the forest. He felt liberated by his poverty and discovered the boundless love of God the Creator.

His behaviour intrigued many young men of his time; some of them decided to follow him. They wore a single long garment

....

3. This summary is adapted from Omer Engelbert. (1979). *St Francis of Assisi: A Biography*. Cincinnati, OH: St. Anthony Messenger Press.

in grey or brown tied with a rope belt with three knots to recall their vows of poverty, chastity and obedience. These brothers travelled the roads together, spreading the good news to the towns and cities they visited.

One day, a wolf was terrorizing the village of Gubbio. The wolf had attacked and eaten livestock and chickens and had seriously injured a man. Filled with love, Francis took it upon himself to settle this conflict: "Brother wolf," he said, "come here. In the name of Christ, I command you not to hurt me or others." The wolf approached him. People were watching from behind the trees. Francis leaned toward the wolf: "Brother wolf, you've done a lot of damage everywhere, killing the creatures of the Lord. You deserve to be tried as a murderer. I want there to be peace between you and the people." Francis understood that the wolf was hungry. He explained to the villagers that they should feed him as one of their own. The wolf agreed. According to legend, he showed signs of subordination and even held out his paw to Francis.

One Easter day, a shepherd gave Francis a lamb as a gift. Needless to say, the sheep received the best of care and faithfully stayed near the saint for many years, even while he was praying.

Francis loved all beings, from the most colourful to the dullest, from the largest to the smallest. When he saw a worm in his path, Francis would pick it up and put it in the grass so it wouldn't be stepped on.

But of all the stories showing that the saint was the brother of all, the story of the birds is the best. One day, as Francis was walking with two brothers near Cannara, he told them, "Stay here while I go preach to our brothers the birds." Birds of many different species were watching him. He addressed them, saying, "My brother birds, be full of thanks to God who has done so much for you! Praise him for your freedom and your beautiful feathers. The Creator must love you very much to give you all of this! Brother birds, do not be ungrateful; sing the praises of the one who gives you so many blessings." While he was speaking, the birds were silent, but as soon as he finished, they began to sing, each according to its talents. Then he blessed them with the sign of the cross and they flew away.

His gentleness and charisma were beyond compare. He drew large crowds and was uncomfortable being the superior of the community. He wanted to visit the Holy Land, and so he boarded a boat with some crusaders. After a fraternal visit to the Muslims, he returned home burdened with two great sorrows: the memory of the massacres the Crusades had caused, and a serious eye disease. He now had to travel around on the back of a donkey.

After a few years, his eye disease had left him nearly blind. He stayed in a dark room most of the time. By candlelight, he wrote a beautiful prayer: the Canticle of the Creatures (see Appendix I). He had asked his brothers that at his death, he be stripped and laid on the ground, to return to God as he had arrived. He died on October 3, 1226, and was canonized two years later.

Saint Kateri Tekakwitha

The story[4] of this saint leads us into the world of the First Nations while maintaining a strong Christian dimension. Kateri was canonized in 2012 – the first North American Aboriginal person to be recognized in this way. She is also the patron saint of ecology.

....

4. This summary is from Juliette Lavergne. (1934). *La vie gracieuse de Catherine Tekakwitha*. Montréal: Editions Albert Lévesque.

Tekakwitha was born in 1656 at Ossernenon in what is now the state of New York. A member of the Turtle Clan, she had a Mohawk father and a Christian Algonquin mother. Little Tekakwitha became an orphan at the age of four, when her parents died of smallpox, a disease brought to the new world by the Europeans. Her little brother also died of the disease; Kateri had smallpox, too, but survived. Her face was covered with scars due to her illness.

She was taken in by her uncle, the village chief. Tekakwitha worked hard, even though her eyesight had been weakened by smallpox. One day, a Black Robe (a Jesuit missionary) came to the village and was allowed to build his own shelter. He told the people the story of Jesus; 12-year-old Kateri was eager to learn more. She listened passionately and soon knew the stories by heart. At age 20, she asked to be baptized. She was given the name Catherine – in Iroquois, Kateri. The people of the village thought she had gone too far. They insulted her, gave her the hardest tasks to do and threw stones at her. However, for her, it was a pleasure to serve the Creator, especially in the most trying moments.

Kateri did not want to get married, and she felt the need to join a Christian clan. Her loyalty, an Aboriginal virtue, was to God, the Great Spirit. Despite the difficulties of the long journey on foot and by canoe, she came at last to Kahnawake (near Montreal).

She liked being alone in the woods and spending time with God there. It was in the forest, among the trees and the silence, that the Great Spirit spoke to her heart. All of nature showed her who the Creator was, and she felt at peace. To be in harmony with all of Creation was a value she had learned from her people since her youth. When the cross became an important symbol in her life, she often tied two sticks together to make a cross.

The example of Jesus who loved us and suffered for us gave her great comfort. She often prayed the rosary, singing it in the Aboriginal style.

Kateri was not afraid to die. For her, it was like coming home. She fell asleep in the Lord during Holy Week, on April 17, 1680. As the trees, plants and animals were given new life, God gave Kateri new life. She was only 24 years old, but was wise beyond her years.

A list of ecological saints

In 1979, Pope John Paul II named Francis of Assisi the patron saint of environmentalists. Many other "ecological saints" are part of our Christian heritage, but not all are well known. Their inspiring attitudes towards God and his Creation make us reflect on our own Christian journey and how we regard Creation. Notice that the following list ends at the 17th century, when Christians came under the influence of Cartesian thought, which caused a rift in humanity's relationship with Creation. Will the 21st century be a period of ecological renaissance for the Church?

Saint (Feast day)	Dates and Country	Brief Anecdote
Paul of Tarsus (January 25)	5–67 Rome	In his letter to the Romans, he wrote: "… the creation itself will be set free from its bondage to decay and will obtain the freedom of the glory of the children of God. We know that the whole creation has been groaning in labour pains until now" (8:21-22).
John the Evangelist (December 27)	11–101 Greece	In the Book of Revelation, he wrote: "You are worthy, our Lord and God, to receive glory and honour and power, for you created all things, and by your will they existed and were created" (4:11). He also had a vision of a new heaven and a new earth.

Saint (Feast day)	Dates and Country	Brief Anecdote
Clement of Rome (November 23)	died ca. 97 Rome	In his letter to the Corinthians (chapter 20), he describes the harmony in Creation: the sun, moon, earth, sea, winds, springs. Then he declares that God wanted peace to reign in his Creation because he desires the good of all his creatures.
Martine of Rome (January 30)	died in 228 Rome	When she was led to the arena to be eaten by a lion, the animal came and lay at her feet. In the end, the emperor had her decapitated. Two eagles stayed near her body until a Christian came and buried her.
Blaise of Sebaste (February 3)	died in 316 Armenia	He was a physician when he was chosen as the bishop of Sebaste. He turned a cave in Mount Argea into his episcopal residence and healed people as well as animals there. He taught so well that even the animals would come and listen to him.
Paul of Thebes (January 15)	died in 345 Egypt	The first hermit, he sought God through contemplation of the desert wilderness. He lived in silence and prayer, having left behind all his possessions. Each day, a crow brought him a piece of bread.
Anthony the Great (January 17)	251–356 Egypt	At the age of 20, he already took the Gospel seriously. He gave all his goods to the poor and went to live in the desert as a hermit. He shared the Good News with all who came to listen, humans and animals alike.
Mary of Egypt (April 2)	died in 421 Egypt	She lived an ascetic life in the desert, in contact with the animals there. When she died, a lion began to dig an appropriate burial place. When it had finished, it turned around and left, gentle as a lamb.
Patrick of Ireland (March 17)	385–461 Ireland	He studied the elements of Celtic spirituality to find in them symbols that could represent a Christian mystery. He chose the shamrock to teach about the Trinity. Some prayers that are attributed to him speak of the elements of nature.

Saint (Feast day)	Dates and Country	Brief Anecdote
Gerasimos of the Jordan (March 5)	died in 475 Israel (Palestine)	One day in the desert, he met a lion suffering from a reed stuck in its paw. The good monk pulled it out and bandaged the wound. For five years, the lion put itself at the monk's service and helped him do his work. They were both vegetarians, eating only figs.
Brigid of Kildare (February 1)	451–525 Ireland	Thanks to her Celtic spirituality, she saw God's goodness in all Creation. The wild ducks flew to her and perched on her hands and shoulders when she called them. This abbess would come out of her monastery to give people braided crosses made from reeds.
Benedict of Nursia (July 11)	480–547 Italy	He wrote the Rule for monastic life, based on a balance between prayer and work (ora et labora). Because the monks had to feed themselves through farming, they had great respect for the rhythms of nature.
Florentius of Nursia (May 23)	died in 548 Italy	Although he lived as a hermit in a cave, he had a hard time being so alone. One day, a huge bear came and lay down at the cave's entrance. By his friendly and gentle demeanour, the animal showed the holy man that he wanted to be his companion. The bear was welcomed joyfully and was trusted to guard the hermit's four sheep.
Columba of Iona (June 9)	521–597 Scotland	This monk took care of animals. One day, he gave special instructions to his brothers to care for a heron that had fallen on the shore after an exhausting flight. He was also fond of a horse that came near to him shortly before he died.
Kevin of Glendalough (June 3)	498–618 Ireland	This hermit prayed exclusively in nature, at the foot of a tree or on a rock. When he prayed in a river, an otter brought him fish to keep up his strength. According to legend, he held a bird's nest in his hands until the eggs hatched.

Saint (Feast day)	Dates and Country	Brief Anecdote
Melangell of Wales (May 27)	died in 641 Wales	This woman was discovered in the woods by a hunter who was following a hare that had run under her dress for protection. The hunter, a prince, was so touched by her holiness that he begged her to found an abbey, in woods that are protected today as an ecological site.
Ghislain of Mons (October 9)	died in 680 Belgium	A large female bear, fleeing from dogs and knights on horseback, sought refuge next to him. He told King Dagobert that the bear had placed herself under God's protection, so the king went away. The bear then took the sack containing the mass kit and fled into the forest. The place where he found the bear became the site of a monastery.
Isaac of Nineveh (January 28)	640–700 Iraq	He was the bishop of Nineveh, but he withdrew to the desert to write, saying, "I want a heart that burns with love for all of Creation, for humans, for birds, for beasts, for demons, for all creatures."
Giles the Hermit (September 1)	died in 720 France	A deer took refuge in his cave and lay down at his feet. An arrow, shot by a furious hunter who was aiming at the deer, pierced the saint's hand instead. King Flavius apologized to the saint. The monk was persuaded to found a monastery in the valley.
Isidore the Farmer (May 15)	1070–1130 Spain	He was a farmer in Madrid all his life. One day, his master discovered him praying in a state of ecstasy, while the oxen continued to pull the plough as if guided by two angels. Amazed at what he saw, his master was converted. He is the patron saint of farmers.
Bernard of Clairvaux (August 20)	1090–1153 France	This Cistercian monk, who founded 72 monasteries, is the author of many books of theology and is a doctor of the Church. "You will find more in the forest than in books. The trees and the rocks will teach you what no master could reveal." He also preserved 20,000 hectares of forest.

Saint (Feast day)	Dates and Country	Brief Anecdote
Hildegard of Bingen (September 17)	1098–1179 Germany	This Benedictine cloistered nun combined scientific observation and mystical contemplation of nature. She studied the properties of plants in order to make medicines. She was also a writer and composer and is recognized as a doctor of the Church.
Francis of Assisi (October 4)	1180–1226 Italy	The Canticle of the Creatures sums up his spirituality: "Be praised, my Lord, through brother Sun … sister Moon and the stars … brother Wind … sister Water … sister our mother Earth …." He also preached to the birds and tamed an enraged wolf that was terrorizing the village of Gubbio.
Clare of Assisi (August 11)	1194–1253 Italy	A disciple of Francis's, she founded the Order of Poor Ladies (also known as the Poor Clares). She lived in extreme simplicity and praised God for everything. She tended a garden so that it became a place of welcome to humans and to birds.
Anthony of Padua (June 13)	1195–1232 Italy	When people didn't listen to him, he began preaching to the fish, naming the gifts God had given them: how God created them, how much freedom he had given them, and how he fed them without their having to work. The fish came close to the shore to listen.
Andrew Segni (February 1)	1230–1302 Italy	As a young Franciscan hermit, he withdrew into a deserted cave far away from everything. The animals of the forest visited him and he became their friend. His most faithful companions were the birds. He spoke to them and the birds responded with their songs.
Roch of Montpellier (August 16)	1340–1379 France	He caught the plague after going on a pilgrimage and then withdrew into the forest. Only a dog came to feed him by bringing him some bread snatched from his master's table every day. Their inseparable bond of friendship gave birth to a popular French expression, "It's Saint Roch and his dog," describing two people who are inseparable.

Saint (Feast day)	Dates and Country	Brief Anecdote
John of the Cross (December 14)	1542–1591 Spain	This monk and mystic preferred contemplation to intellectual analysis. "The fly that lands on honey can no longer fly, and the soul that [thinks too much] is no longer free for contemplation." He often prayed in nature.
Kateri Tekakwitha (April 17)	1656–1680 Canada	It was in the forest, among the trees and the silence, that the Great Spirit spoke to her heart. All of nature spoke to her of the Creator, and she felt at peace. Being in harmony with all Creation was a value she had learned from a young age among the Aboriginal people.

Suggested Activities

- Display an image of one of the above-mentioned ecological saints along with a description of his or her life and connection to the environment on a bulletin board in the church or on the parish or diocesan website on the saint's feast day. For example, the week before April 17, you could display a picture of Kateri Tekakwitha and her story.

- Make up a game where players must match the name, the life story and the picture with a particular ecological saint. This is a fun way for all ages to learn how these faith witnesses lived in relationship with God's Creation.

- Do some research and prepare a short testimonial about an ecological saint, then dress in costume to tell the saint's story. Bring to life the story of this witness, allowing him or her to speak to us and guide us today.

PERSONAL NOTES

Eucharistic Prayers and Creation

The Greek word *eucharistia* (εὐχαριστία) means "thanksgiving" – not only for our own life, but also for the presence of God in the life of the community and for the life that God breathes into his Creation.

The Eucharistic liturgy is, surprisingly, a fertile source of environmental awareness. The liturgy has its roots in the ancient Greek and Semitic cultures, which saw their environment as the result of the creative work of God. This is evident in two commonly used parts of the Eucharistic Prayers: the prayer for the preparation of the gifts, and the prayer immediately following the Sanctus in Eucharistic Prayer III.

Prayer for the preparation of the gifts

> Blessed are you, Lord God of all creation,
> for through your goodness we have received
> the bread we offer you;
> fruit of the earth and work of human hands,
> it will become for us the bread of life.
>
> Blessed are you, Lord God of all creation,
> for through your goodness we have received
> the wine we offer you;
> fruit of the vine and work of human hands,
> it will become our spiritual drink.

These two prayers stem from the Jewish prayer of blessing for the bread that has been sung for centuries during the Sabbath and the Passover supper: "Blessed are You, Lord our God, King of the universe, who brings forth bread from the earth." That this ritual meal is organized every year in spring, when nature is reborn, makes the need to give thanks to God even more meaningful. If God no longer provided for us, we could not eat bread, "fruit of the earth," and drink wine, "fruit of the vine." Both are also the result of human labour, a sign that human beings are co-creators with God. Holding the bread in our hands, we marvel that humankind is able to care for the earth and make it even more bountiful.

Knowing that this blessing is so essential, can we just turn our backs and not be mindful of the ecological crisis? God can give us bread and wine, provided there is an ecological balance. But if the soil is impoverished and climate change threatens the harvest, soon nothing will grow and the responsibility will be ours.

Bread

For the apostles sitting around the table with Jesus at the Last Supper, bread was the product of the land (wheat), the result of human labour and their daily food. Jesus added another level of meaning to the bread: his body given for us.

Can we, as Christians, allow the bread of which we partake, the body of Christ, to be made of wheat grown with the use of pesticides and chemical fertilizers? Pesticides can cause cancer,

and the run-off from chemical fertilizers upsets the chemical balance in many lakes, causing blue-green algae, for example. But there is good news: more and more parishes and dioceses insist that the hosts they use are made from organically grown wheat. In 2012, the Sisters of Saint Clare in Valleyfield, Quebec, agreed to use only organic flour in the making of altar breads, a first in Canada!

Wine

For the apostles sitting around the table with Jesus, the wine made from grapes was the product of the vine, the result of human labour, and a drink for celebrations. Jesus added another level of meaning to the wine: his blood shed for us.

So, Jesus took the daily food of bread, and he took the drink reserved for special occasions: wine. This wine, in all likelihood, was produced locally or regionally. It was transported to market in a cart pulled by a donkey. Today, wine can travel great distances before arriving at our table. In eastern Canada, almost all parishes use an altar wine from California, 4,000 kilometres away. The farther it travels, the more greenhouse gases are emitted by the trucks carrying it, which traps heat in the atmosphere and leads to radical changes in climate. The place of origin of the wine we buy has an impact on the quality of life of future generations. Parishes and dioceses can consider buying wine from local or regional vineyards. The *Côtes d'Ardoise* vineyard in Dunham, Quebec, for example, offers both a red and a white wine that were officially approved as sacramental wine by the bishop of Saint-Hyacinthe in May 2011.

Eucharistic Prayer III (following the *Sanctus*)

66 You are indeed Holy, O Lord,
and all you have created
rightly gives you praise,
for through your Son our Lord Jesus Christ,
by the power and working of the Holy Spirit,
you give life to all things and make them holy... 99

The assertion that Creation gives praise to God is not some modern New Age concept. It is rooted in an ancient Christian cosmology, where the existence of each creature is desired by God, because it is God who gives life. In exchange, the creatures show their gratitude by praising God in their own way: a flower's beauty, a bird's song, the graceful swimming of a beluga. But in the face of the current biodiversity crisis, how should we understand this part of the Eucharistic Prayer?

It has become difficult to keep track of the number of species disappearing from the surface of the Earth at the overwhelming rate of 100 per day! The loss of life on Earth is accelerating. Many species disappear even before they are discovered. The total number of species is well over a million. For about 41,000 species of flora and fauna being monitored by biologists, over 16,000 are included in varying degrees on the list of endangered species, according to the World Conservation Union – nearly 40 percent. Human activity appears to be directly or indirectly responsible for these disappearances, through the decline in natural habitats, the increase in pollution, climate change, uncontrolled hunting, introduction of invasive species, and the list goes on.

In Quebec, the Ministry of Sustainable Development, the Environment and Parks has already recorded the total extinction of three animal species: the Common Eider Duck, the Great Auk and the Passenger Pigeon. This means there are no longer any of these birds remaining on Earth. These species have been wiped out mainly due to overhunting, which is not a natural phenomenon.

So, in the Eucharistic Prayer, we join our praise with that of existing creatures, but what about those that no longer praise God? "All you have created rightly gives you praise," we say – well, not quite all, as many have disappeared for good. We have two choices: revise the text of the liturgy or promote the profound ecological message of this prayer. I am in favour of the second option.

Deepening our understanding of these prayers will make our Christian communities more aware of the need to stand up and protect our natural environments. Remember that the Eucharistic Prayer is not restricted to personal salvation, but is of cosmic significance!

Virtues as Environmental Values

Environmental education has attempted to define environmental values. My research of the literature in this area revealed that these values have never been defined. What is even more surprising is that educators and researchers haven't found an adequate answer, either. Those involved in environmental education (schools, museums, governments, charitable organizations and others) use the term "environmental values," but it is not always easy to know what these are. What are the key environmental values?

A Small-Group Exercise: Identifying Environmental Values

Write down the spontaneous answers of the people in the group to these two questions.

> **1** **What are the different values associated with the environmental movement?**
>
> **Responses may include these ideas:**
>
> Reduce consumption; reduce, reuse, recycle; conserve heating and car fuel; *simplicity.*
>
> Foresee the consequences of mining; manage nuclear waste; *prudence.*
>
> Make changes in environmental practices and stick with them; make new transportation habits; *perseverance.*
>
> Buy fair trade products; protest the impact of pollution on the poor; *fairness.*

Note: "Values" are identified here by actions and behaviours, because people generally find it difficult to express values such as simplicity, fairness, solidarity, etc.

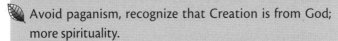

② For Christians, what values would need to be added to the environmental movement?

Responses may include these ideas:

🍃 Avoid paganism, recognize that Creation is from God; more spirituality.

🍃 Avoid promoting alarmist discussions; counteract the sense of despair by proposing hopeful solutions.

🍃 Promote human solidarity, communion with Creation and love for the world.

The virtues

An educational researcher, Mario Salomone,[5] made a bold proposal: the four cardinal virtues – temperance, prudence, courage and justice – inform our research of environmental values. These virtues, which the Church has promoted for hundreds of years, provide an excellent point of reference for an environmental ethic. These virtues correspond to the list derived from the group exercise described above.

........................,

5. Mario Salomone. (2006). "Under the Sign of Saint Francis: Catholics, Ethics of Responsibility, and Environmental Education," *Canadian Journal of Environmental Education, 11* (1), 74–87.

Ecological values can take their inspiration from the four **cardinal virtues**. Seen from an ecological perspective, here they are:

TEMPERANCE calls for moderation, the search for balance in the use of environmental resources; it respects the limits of ecosystems, halts all forms of waste and is content with a simpler lifestyle.

PRUDENCE means acting responsibly when making everyday decisions, with due consideration of their consequences: caution is a related concept.

COURAGE strengthens us to face the challenge of an ecological conversion and to persevere when we adopt new habits.

JUSTICE requires a fair distribution of goods among all humans and respects the order of the universe.

The three **theological virtues**, which are the fruit of God's Word, are the Church's greatest contribution to the ecological movement:

FAITH allows us to see the environment as God's Creation and promotes a theocentric rather than an anthropocentric or pagan approach.

HOPE sustains a positive and motivational environmental outlook – much more helpful than a doom-and-gloom point of view, which can lead to despair;

LOVE (charity) for the world leads to taking care of Creation in order to turn people away from selfishness and a desire for excessive comfort and towards the needs of others.

In teaching environmental values, the Church becomes a major partner in solving the environmental crisis. Through educational activities featuring these values, the Church fulfills its mission (to preach the Gospel) and promotes the mission of the environmental movement (to raise awareness). Because they are both ecological and evangelical, the virtues could also be called "ecoevangelical values"!

PERSONAL NOTES

PERSONAL NOTES

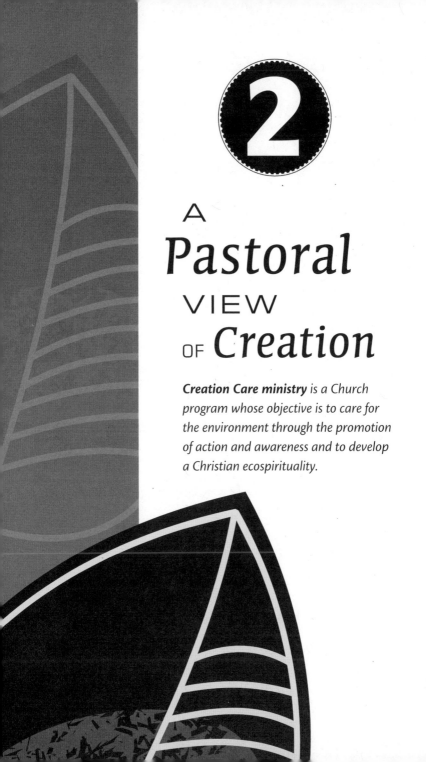

2

A

Pastoral

VIEW

OF *Creation*

Creation Care ministry is a Church program whose objective is to care for the environment through the promotion of action and awareness and to develop a Christian ecospirituality.

Pastoral ministry in the Church

Pastoral ministry follows the model of Jesus the Good Shepherd, as illustrated, for example, in his encounter with the disciples of Emmaus: he walks with them, shares their experiences, helps them better understand the meaning of the Scriptures, eats with them, and inspires them to witness to God's actions. In the same way, the minister who prepares families for the baptism of a child walks with the parents on the road to baptism. The youth minister cares for the spiritual needs of young people. Those in hospital chaplaincy accompany the sick and dying through various stages of their journey. In social ministry, the pastoral worker is concerned with the poor and others who are in need of social justice.

All these ministries involve teaching, action and celebration. Just as we marvel when we see a newborn baby, Creation Care ministry helps us marvel at the beauty of nature. As pastoral care in hospitals supports people who are sick or dying, Creation Care ministry supports endangered ecosystems. And as social ministry defends victims of injustice, Creation Care ministry defends people and creatures who are vulnerable to the consequences of ecological destruction.

Taking care of God's Creation

When it comes to the environment, we are inundated with terminology: the environment, natural resources, ecology, sustainable development, green – these are only a few of the words we hear. Any of these choices could have been used to designate this new form of ministry that is concerned with protecting our environment, but none of them seemed right. What expression would be most suitable for Christians speaking about the environment?

The term *Creation Care* was chosen for this new type of minis-try. Indeed, plants and animals are creatures, the work of God. Environmental problems are a threat to the integrity of Creation, and as Christians we must intervene. Destroying Creation is irresponsible, because it is through Creation that the Creator transmits and sustains all life. In short, any action that does not allow Creation to regenerate, to remain sustainable, should be denounced. Every area that has been devastated by pollution should be restored, which would bring "good news to the whole creation" (Mark 16:15).

While reading these words, you may think that you are not to blame for the state of the environment, because you are not directly responsible for clear-cutting or the melting of the Arctic sea ice, the mistreatment of farm animals or the pollu-tion discharged in mining and other kinds of irresponsible treatment of the environment. But in fact, we all share this responsibility, as we all use paper, drive a car, eat meat, purchase battery-operated devices, and so on. The sum of these actions leaves a huge environmental footprint that can be reduced when we make changes in our daily behaviour. As an individual, you shouldn't take all the blame, but all of us are partly responsible.

To help us shoulder our responsibility, the Church has devel-oped this new ministry, Creation Care, to build community awareness of environmental issues, take action in the parish, diocese, convent or monastery to reduce its environmental footprint, and help the community rediscover Christian ecospirituality. We serve God when we care for Creation.

In communion with the universal Church

Creation Care is a new ministry that is still developing in the Catholic Church in Canada. In northern Italy, however, several Catholic dioceses, such as Brescia and Venice, carry out this type of ministry under the title of *Pastorale del Creato*. In Germany, Catholic churches have had *umweltbeauftragte* (ministers of the environment) since the 1990s, especially in the dioceses of Munich and Berlin. In Canada and the United Church, the Anglican Church and other Reformed churches have developed the ministry called Creation Care. In the Canadian Catholic Church, Creation Care ministry is in continuity with these churches throughout the world. It is a sacred call that is being heard in more and more places. The diocese of Saint-Jean-Longueuil was the first Canadian diocese to appoint a diocesan officer for Creation Care ministry, in 2011.

The Three Pillars of Creation Care Ministry

In order for Creation Care ministry to be effective, it must reach the various activities of a faith community. These are supported by three pillars:

SPIRITUALITY: By contemplating Creation and celebrating our Creator, we enter into a relationship with the creatures around us and love them as God loves them. This pillar is particularly linked to liturgy and catechesis.

AWARENESS: By explaining and informing people about environmental issues such as climate change and the biodiversity crisis, these issues may be better understood. This pillar particularly affects parish activities outside of Sunday liturgies, as well as communication through the parish bulletin, website and other announcements.

ACTION: By improving the energy efficiency of its buildings, recycling, cleaning with environmentally friendly products, maintaining the grounds without using pesticides, choosing sustainable means of transportation and serving locally grown and fair trade food, we reduce the environmental footprint of the Christian community. This pillar particularly affects church administrators and the custodian, but can also touch larger numbers of parishioners at church gatherings.

Christian Ecospirituality

Introduction

Christian ecospirituality draws extensively on Franciscan spirituality, but is also inspired by Saint Kateri Tekakwitha, Saint Kevin, Saint Benedict, and many other saints. What makes this kind of spirituality unique is that it is connected in communion and worship with other creatures. It does not worship the creatures themselves (which would be pagan practice) or our own creations (which would be idolatry). Instead, Christian ecospirituality recognizes the wisdom in God's Creation and strives to keep it in balance. This spiritual sense is nourished by the contemplation of nature, such as in a park or a garden.

Success stories

"Communion with Creation"

This activity focuses on the *spirituality* pillar and enables people to rediscover a Creation-inspired spirituality.

One morning a couple of years ago, around 30 parishioners – of all ages – gathered in St. Marguerite Bourgeoys church in Longueuil, Quebec, to explore the connection between the Eucharist and the environment.

After a word of welcome, the organizer turned over the mike to a speaker from Guardians of Creation, an organization that offers tools for a pastoral approach to Creation in the Church.[6]

....

6. Guardians of Creation is a group of speakers who specialize in ecospirituality. They are available to speak in churches and at events. See http://www.gardienscreation.org/index.php?lang=en. I founded this organization in 2005 to offer a Christian response to the environmental crisis.

The talk on "Communion with Creation" revealed the strong environmental character of certain parts of the Eucharistic Prayers of the Mass. For example, as we saw earlier, the simple prayer over the gifts of bread and wine reminds us that God provides for us from the earth and from human hands. Pondering the meaning of these prayers carries the liturgy of the Eucharist beyond the single aspect of personal salvation and opens it up to the community and to all of Creation. After the talk and a discussion period, participants entered into the Eucharist in a new way.

The words of the liturgy had not been rewritten. Rather, praying the prayers in a new light allowed people to hear them in a renewed way. The participants said they would never hear the prayers in the same way again, as they now had a deeper meaning. Also, the choice had been made to use bread made with organic flour and a local wine. The group was convinced that, following the example of Saint Francis of Assisi, each Eucharist can renew and deepen our communion with Creation.

"Making Connections"

This activity also focuses on the pillar of *spirituality*. It supports the encounter with the Creator through contemplation of Creation.

It took place on a beautiful autumn afternoon at Saint Francis of Assisi church in eastern Montreal with a group of 40 participants, made up of youth and their parents.

The session began with a short presentation on the story of the first human (as told in Genesis 2). The facilitator followed up by saying:

> The first man was fashioned from the earth, water and air. 'Adam' is not some supernatural being set down on the planet, but a created being made from the surrounding natural elements. Our human physical make-up confirms this, because we are made of earth (food), water (beverages) and air (breath). We are an extension of our environment, and our environment is, in a way, an extension of ourselves, so we are in many ways linked together, part of each other.

Participants were then invited to go outside and contemplate something from God's Creation in nature (such as a cloud, a tree, an ant, a bird, a squirrel). After about 15 minutes, they came back inside and spoke of what they had discovered. Their comments were touching:

> Wow, I never knew there was so much life crawling around on the ground!

> The bird flew onto a branch, then dropped down a few branches as if it were coming to see me. That warmed my heart.

> I stayed near a tree and admired its patience. It was so firmly rooted in the ground. I would like to have such unshakable strength.

After this moment of connection with Creation, the facilitator recalled a few of the stories about Saint Francis of Assisi. Through these stories, the young people were able to identify with a saint whose connection to all of God's creatures was a major part of his faith. The gathering ended with the Canticle of the Creatures.

Other Ways of Developing Christian Ecospirituality

On a practical level, Christian ecospirituality fits very well into the educational programs and prayer life of the community. Here are some suggestions for incorporating this kind of spirituality into your community:

- Integrate education on Creation Care into each year's catechetical sessions for young people;

- Highlight the theme of Creation in homilies, especially following the frequent Scripture readings that evoke this theme;

- Stress the ecologically related Eucharistic Prayers during Mass to open hearts to God's Creation;

- Insert an intention on caring for Creation in the Prayer of the Faithful;

- Have the liturgy committee organize, at least twice a year, a Sunday celebration on the theme of Creation. This could be during harvest in the fall (Thanksgiving) and during planting in the spring (Rogation).

- Offer a Lenten retreat on the theme of ecological conversion.

- Organize prayer afternoons or evenings on special days, such as Earth Hour, World Water Day, and other appropriate times.

For helpful readings, prayers and liturgies, visit www.GreenChurch.ca.

Raising Environmental Awareness in the Church

Introduction

Environmental awareness is necessary in the Christian community because we must first open our minds to learning about an issue before opening our hearts and taking action. You have probably donated to a charity like Development and Peace when you became aware of suffering somewhere in the world and you wanted to help. Christians cannot commit to working for a more sustainable world without first raising awareness in their faith community. Keep in mind that we play a role in the coming of the Kingdom of God (Philippians 1:6).

Success stories

"Ecological Footprint" activity

This activity focuses on the pillar of *awareness*, to help members of the faith community understand why it is important to take care of Creation.

This activity took place at St. Anne parish in Chicoutimi, Quebec, several years ago. After the Sunday liturgy, people gathered for a brunch featuring local foods.

At the end of the meal, the facilitator explained the schedule of activities. First, everyone completed a worksheet measuring the ecological footprint of each person in their family. This took some time. They calculated the number of planet Earths required to sustain their current level of consumption. The average number was five planet Earths.

Then they were asked to write their results on a piece of footprint-shaped cardboard. Next they identified changes they could make to their day-to-day choices and activities to reduce their ecological footprint (such as carpooling more often and using less hot water).

The activity concluded with small-group discussions about adopting more environmentally friendly practices at home and at church. The parish Green Team took note of the suggestions made for the church.

Movie and discussion

This activity also centres on the *awareness* pillar; it helps members of the Christian community to readjust their outlook on Creation.

This activity took place at St. Charles Borromée church in Quebec City a couple of years ago and was part of a broader program in the Fairtrade Fortnight (always held during the first two weeks of May).

Participants were invited to arrive at the church a few minutes before the screening so they would have time to drink fair trade coffee, buy fair trade products and visit the Development and Peace kiosk. After the call to be seated, the lights went out and the church was transformed into a movie theatre for two hours. People attentively watched the documentary film *Home*, produced by Yann Arthus-Bertrand in 2009. (This movie is free of charge and downloadable from the Internet.) It begins with some amazing images displaying the beauty of our planet, followed by scenes of overexploited and polluted areas; the film ends with images showing possible solutions.

The ensuing discussion was lively, because we had to find the balance between the exploitation of natural resources for our needs and the protection of natural environments for the needs of other creatures. "God allows us to take whatever we need, but not whatever we want," said one participant. "I now understand ecojustice a little better; my actions here can affect another continent," said another. Someone else simply summarized,

> It helped me realize how beautiful and fragile our Earth is; that it is our only home. I want to take care of it.

Then a theological aspect was added to the discussion:

> I believe God is calling me, calling us, to take care of the Earth, his Creation. 'Business as usual' is unacceptable to God. That is why he calls modern prophets to speak out against certain situations.

More ways to build awareness for Creation Care

On a practical level, environmental awareness can be developed through action and through published suggestions. Here are some examples:

- Publish a "Green Tip" in the parish bulletin and on the website every week.

- Allocate a section of the bulletin board for announcing environmental campaigns, such as the Nature Challenge or other local events.

- Invite a speaker to talk about an environmental theme (such as water, climate, biodiversity) and engage with participants through a question period. Encourage participants to commit to adopting environmentally friendly habits. Involve the youth!

- Watch a documentary about an environmental issue (such as genetically modified seeds, fossil fuels, boreal forests).

- Show a film that highlights the beauty of Creation (such as Nat Geo Movies from National Geographic, or the Planet Earth series).

- Host a community event that brings together members of the parish or diocese and members of environmental groups, such as an eco-artisan fair.

- Organize members of the faith community to take part in an environmental demonstration. Invite them to make some original posters with slogans like "We care for Creation" and "God saw that it was very good (Genesis 1:32)."

More suggestions and campaigns can be found at www.GreenChurch.ca.

Environmental Action in the Church

Introduction

Action is the result of awareness and spirituality – the first two pillars in Creation Care. Imagine the contradiction of a faith community that preaches the integrity of Creation, but serves its meals on disposable plates, sprays pesticides on the lawn and doesn't repair leaky faucets. As Jesus said, we know a tree by its fruit! Our Church today must not only pray to the Creator, but must also take care of Creation. Aware of the challenges posed by changing our behaviour, Pope John Paul II did not hesitate to speak of "ecological conversion."[7] Some decisions are easy to put into practice, while others involve costly sacrifices and take time to achieve. But our Christian tradition knows the value of sacrifice that leads to grace.

Success Stories

Cleaning a park near the church

This activity focuses on the *action* pillar of Creation Care and engages the church in reducing the environmental footprint of its neighbourhood.

In a Montreal park near St. Kevin church a couple of years ago, some 20 members of the church community joined 150 of their neighbours in picking up litter in the park. While the cleanup

....

7. Pope John Paul II, General Audience, January 17, 2001. http://www. vatican.va/holy_father/john_paul_ii/audiences/2001/documents/ hf_jp-ii_aud_20010117_en.html

was organized by the city, the pastoral team thought it was a good idea to encourage parishioners to become involved in the name of their faith.

The activity was announced from the pulpit, in the parish bulletin and on posters at the entrance to the church more than a month before the event. Once participants were onsite, city officials handed out gloves, garbage bags and even t-shirts that people could keep. Participants remarked that "it is great to see so many people caring for Creation together."

Fundraising for compact fluorescent light bulbs

This activity is also centred on the pillar of *action* and aims at reducing the church's consumption of electricity, which in turn reduces the impact on the environment (while saving money on the electric bill!).

It took place a few years ago at Beaconsfield United Church in Quebec, under the banner of "Save Creation one bulb at a time."

Around 200 members of the community came to the church on a fall Sunday to contemplate the artistic representation of a leafless tree on the wall. After the greeting at the beginning of the celebration, the head of this fundraising campaign explained that the tree with bare branches could become greener in the coming weeks as the inefficient light bulbs (about 180) in all the rooms of the church were replaced with compact fluorescent light bulbs (CFLs). What are the benefits? CFLs use four times less energy than incandescent bulbs and last six times longer, creating less waste. And when they eventually burn out, they will be recycled so that the mercury they contain can be used to make another CFL bulb.

Every week, people saw the tree and remembered to contribute $8 (the cost of a CFL). In exchange, they were given a green leaf to stick on a branch of the tree. A leafy green tree began to emerge, the church premises consumed less and less energy, and people adopted the expression "Save Creation." They were so caught up in this project that they purchased CFLs for their homes as well... proof that green behaviour in the Church can extend beyond the walls of the church.

More ways of taking action for Creation Care

A range of practical ecological improvements can be made in a church, convent or monastery.

The building's energy efficiency

- Illuminate the church's tower until midnight, not all night.
- Change the interior lighting so it consumes less energy.
- Improve the insulation around the windows and doors.
- Do an energy audit of the church and improve the insulation of the walls and roof, if needed.
- Study the various sources of energy – oil, natural gas, electric, geothermal, solar – and evaluate which one(s) would be most efficient in your setting.

Sustainable transportation

- Install bike racks near the entrance to the church.
- Indicate in the parish bulletin and on the website which bus routes pass near the church.
- Organize carpooling for Sunday masses.

- Organize a blessing for alternative means of transportation – such as bicycles, roller blades and skateboards – during "Clean Air Day" in early June, for example.

Water consumption

- Place a small sign with the words "Praise to you, Lord, for our Sister Water" near the faucets.
- Install signs saying "bottled water–free zone."
- Repair leaky faucets.
- When renovating washrooms, replace toilets with low-flush models.

Cleaning products

- For cleaning windows, use a mixture of one part vinegar and four parts water. Economical and ecological!
- Make your own biodegradable cleaning products to avoid using chemicals.
- Purchase certified ecological cleaning products; the word "green" on the label does not always mean ecological.

Waste reduction (reduce, reuse, recycle)

- Reduce the use of paper (e.g., use a projector to avoid printing hymns for liturgies).
- Encourage the reuse of linens, office furniture and other items you no longer need by donating them to a thrift store or holding an annual bazaar.
- Recycle paper, metal, glass and plastic by placing recycling bins in handy areas;
- Recycle ink from printer cartridges as well as batteries, cellphones and bread fasteners to generate funds for worthy causes.

- Compost food waste by taking part in municipal composting programs or by installing a compost bin on church property.

Environmentally friendly eating habits

- Buy fair trade tea and coffee for meetings and gatherings.

- Choose organic and/or locally grown food for your community suppers and write this information on signs so everyone knows where the food came from.

- Encourage local purchases. Some churches organize "100-mile lunches" where all the ingredients come from within that radius. The group learns more about the availability of local products and has a delicious meal!

- For the Eucharist, choose hosts and wine from local and/or organic sources.

Grounds maintenance

- Plant milkweed to help the monarch butterfly to reproduce.

- Let a portion of the land grow "wild" for the use of local wildlife.

- Install birdhouses to hear the birds singing their praises around the church.

- Avoid the use of pesticides and chemical fertilizers. Promote the use of natural alternatives.

- Replace the grass lawn with clover and/or thyme, which require no mowing or watering.

A detailed list of environmental actions and practices is available at www.GreenChurch.ca.

Ten Steps to Greening Your Church

1 **Create a Green Team:** Invite members of your faith community (including at least one young person) to be part of a Green Team. Make a list of ecological improvements you have already made and celebrate them. Then hold a brainstorming session to identify ways you can promote environmental awareness among church members. The Green Church program (www.GreenChurch.ca) can help you get started!

2 **Develop an environmental policy:** Every serious institution in the 21st century needs an environmental policy that directs purchases, waste management and other decisions. Make sure your faith community is on board!

3 **Offer "green tips":** It is so easy to include "green tips" in the parish bulletin or on the diocesan website. Adding these bits of information about how we can respect and protect the environment is important to the community and stimulates personal involvement.

4 **Start small:** Church culture doesn't change overnight, so you will probably have to take baby steps at the beginning. Most churches start by placing recycling bins in all the rooms or introducing compact fluorescent lighting.

5 **Make an action plan:** All your resolutions are well intentioned, but each one must have a deadline and someone in charge. It is better to spread out the project over time so no one becomes exhausted and the new ways of doing things can become regular habits.

6 **Emphasize the spiritual dimension:** Talk about the new environmental focus in a Sunday homily. When more and more people realize that protecting the environment is a scriptural value, Creation Care will grow.

7 **Raise awareness:** Some churches invite a keynote speaker or show a documentary film to stimulate discussion. Others organize a series of classes on faith and the environment. It is also helpful to take part in awareness-raising campaigns.

8 **Partner with your neighbourhood:** We reach more people and accomplish more when we partner with others instead of trying to blaze our own trail. Some churches organize an annual eco-fair that involves local groups.

9 **Share your vision:** Write a story for the local media, make a documentary, paint a mural, or speak in a school or to a group of seniors. Let others know what you are doing so they can get involved and this important mission can grow.

10 **Celebrate!** Plan to celebrate God's Creation in prayer two to four times a year. Prepare special liturgies that integrate prayer, awareness and a promise of action. In the summer, celebrate an outdoor liturgy to enjoy the beauty and fullness of God's Creation.

PERSONAL NOTES

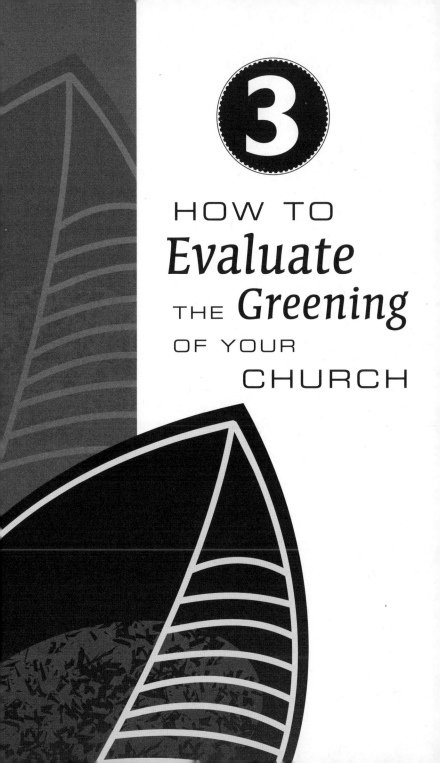

3

HOW TO
Evaluate
THE *Greening*
OF YOUR
CHURCH

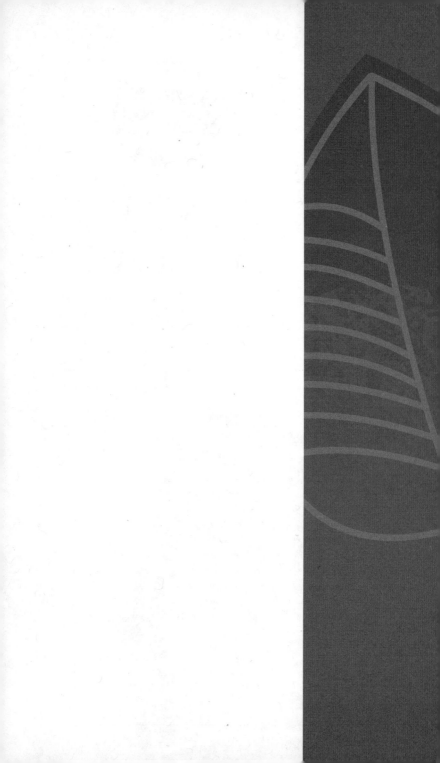

Prepare an annual report

Here are some questions you can ask to assess the gradual transformation of your faith community as it moves towards taking better care of Creation. With the three pillars of Creation Care in mind, three basic questions may be asked:

- Is our faith community living a spirituality that is in closer communion with God's Creation?

- Has our faith community become more aware of environmental issues?

- Has our faith community reduced its ecological footprint?

The following questions are only benchmarks, so do not hesitate to remove some or to add others. Review them together during a Green Team meeting.

Spirituality

- How many Sundays were dedicated to the theme of Creation?
- How many homilies referred to the environment?
- How many catechesis meetings were on the theme of Creation?
- Other issues:

_____

_____

_____

_____

_____

_____

Awareness

- Have you inserted "green tips" in the weekly bulletin?
- Which environmental groups did your community partner with?
- Which environmental campaigns did you promote?
- Which activities helped build environmental awareness in the faith community? (movies, speakers, eco-fair, etc.)
- Other issues:

_____

_____

_____

_____

_____

_____

_____

_____

_____

_____

_____

_____

_____

_____

_____

_____

_____

Action

- What type of heating do you have at the church (oil, gas, electricity, heat pump, geothermal)?
- How have you improved energy efficiency (lighting and energy efficient appliances, better insulation)?
- Do you organize carpooling at the church?
- Do you buy fair trade, organic or local products?
- Do you use environmentally friendly cleaning products?
- Have you reduced your water consumption?
- Are you using sustainable (not disposable) tableware? Do you recycle enough (paper, containers, glass)?
- Does your landscaping and grounds maintenance reflect a concern for Creation?
- Other issues:

_____

_____

_____

_____

_____

_____

_____

_____

_____

_____

_____

_____

PERSONAL NOTES

CONCLUSION

This practical guide for Creation Care ministry was designed so that dioceses, parishes and religious communities can take tangible steps towards a theology of Creation. Thanks to your pastoral involvement, our Church will increase its praise to our Father and Creator and will affirm its role in protecting Creation. In this way, the Good News will be proclaimed "to every creature under heaven" (Colossians 1:23).

Official mandates

Creation Care ministry must be present at all the different hierarchical levels of our Church. Dioceses, parishes and religious communities play a role in this new ministry. With respect to ecclesial order and to apostolic tradition, the mandate of Creation Care ministry is conferred first of all on the bishop. To carry out this ministry in his diocese, he appoints Creation Care officers at diocesan and parish levels. Superiors of religious congregations entrust this ministry to someone in each of their houses or monasteries.

Diocesan officer for Creation Care ministry

At the diocesan level, someone in a full-time position can be responsible for this department. The Creation Care officer will

- organize a yearly training session so that staff are kept informed about useful tools and materials and have a refresher course on the theme of Creation;

- publicize news about this ministry in Church media (parish bulletins, Catholic newspapers and magazines, etc.) and the secular media (newspapers, radio, TV, Internet, etc.);

- establish an annual Creation Sunday and invite all the parishes in the diocese to observe this day with a special liturgy on the theme of Creation;

- network with local environmental groups to keep up to date on current environmental issues and solutions, and make a list of these groups available to members of the pastoral staff;

- inform the faithful about environmental awareness campaigns to get them involved;

- Become a resource person whom parish councils may consult about alternative energy sources and other energy-saving solutions.

Parish officer for Creation Care ministry (or Creation Care minister)

At the parish level, the responsibility for Creation Care is shared by the entire pastoral team (clergy and laity), but one person is appointed as Creation Care minister (with the equivalent salary of one day per week) to coordinate the activities during the year. The main tasks are

- working with the various committees (such as liturgy, catechesis and social justice) and the parish council to carry out activities touching all three pillars (action, awareness and spirituality) of Creation Care;

- contacting a local environmental group to propose church participation and cooperation (e.g., in a campaign or environmental event);

- supporting the parish Green Team (or establishing one);
- organizing two to four Sunday liturgies per year on the theme of Creation;
- networking with the diocesan Creation Care officer to share information and to stimulate the involvement of the faithful;
- publicizing ecological activities and disseminating green tips and useful information through the church bulletin website.

Creation Care minister in a religious community

Creation Care ministry should be one of the ministries of religious congregations (apostolic, missionary, contemplative, or other). The amount of time devoted to this ministry will vary, depending on the size of the community and the other ministries it carries out. Creation Care responsibilities in a religious community's provincial or regional headquarters may be similar to those at the diocesan level; those in a local community or monastery may be similar to what happens at the parish level.

A contemplative community might organize a retreat on Christian ecospirituality, especially if it is situated on beautiful grounds that inspire wonder in the contemplation of nature.

Environmental awareness and involvement could easily be linked to the charisms of many missionary and apostolic congregations.

All communities will need to implement ways of reducing the environmental impact of the community and thus bear witness that loving God means taking care of Creation.

Formation

The Green Church program offers a one-day training session for church staff (clergy and pastoral assistants) as well as interested volunteers. This course allows time for discussion, workshops and games. It also offers concrete tools referring to each of the three pillars (spirituality, awareness and action) of Creation Care. Contact the Canadian Centre for Ecumenism (www.oikoumene.ca) to book this training in your area.

In the near future, faculties of theology and training institutes will offer courses on Creation Care ministry to train pastoral staff who are interested in taking up this ministry. Online courses will no doubt be available.

The fruits of hope

Some positive results of this ministry are obvious: parishes reduce their environmental impact, the ecological footprint of individuals in the community is reduced, environmental issues are better understood, a Christian ecological spirituality is being renewed. But other unexpected results have also appeared: young people are getting involved in Green Teams, some projects have fostered Christian unity and dialogue, green projects have received positive coverage in the media, and environmental groups are feeling more hopeful.

This practical guide is meant to serve as a cornerstone to help support the construction of something new inside our Church so that it may always be faithful to Christ and to the inspiration of the Holy Spirit in our time. Many see it as a "sign of the times."

May God our Father, Creator of heaven and earth, God who loves everything he has created and who is the source of all life, bless this new ministry. Amen.

PERSONAL NOTES

PERSONAL NOTES

APPENDIX I

The Canticle of the Creatures

Written by Saint Francis of Assisi in 1224

Most High, all-powerful and good Lord,
all praise is yours, all glory, all honor and all blessing.
To you, alone, Most High, do they belong.
No man is worthy to pronounce your name.

All praise be yours, my Lord,
through all you have made,
and first my lord Brother Sun, who brings the day;
and through whom you give us light.
How beautiful is he, how radiant in all his splendor;
Of you, Most High, he bears the likeness.

All Praise be yours, my Lord, through Sister Moon
and the stars; in the heavens you have made them,
bright, and precious, and fair.
All praise be yours, my Lord,
through Brothers wind and air, and fair and stormy,
all the weather's moods,
by which you cherish all that you have made.

All praise be yours, my Lord, through Sister Water,
so useful, humble, precious and pure.
All praise be yours, my Lord, through Brother Fire,
through whom you brighten up the night.
How beautiful is he, how cheerful!
Full of power and strength.

All praise be yours, my Lord, through our Sister
Mother Earth, who sustains us and governs us,
and produces various fruits with colored flowers and herbs.
Praise and bless my Lord, and give him thanks
And serve him with great humility.

Saint Francis of Assisi composed this poem, which many consider the most beautiful of the Italian language, towards the end of his life. He was nearly blind and very ill because of the stigmata (wounds on his hands, feet and stomach). He spent his time in a small, dark room. It was in this darkness that he composed this hymn of praise to the Creator, based on his past observations of the heavenly bodies and the four elements. He later added a verse about forgiveness and another about our sister death.

APPENDIX II

Calendar of Christian Feasts and Environmental Days

This chart will help you find dates for organizing events on the theme of Creation.

Date	Feast or Event	Actions to take
January (3rd week)	Week of Prayer for Christian Unity	Partner with another church to organize a talk or a prayer service on the theme of Creation.
February 14	Saint Valentine	Raise awareness about labour practices and exploitation and offer a selection of fair trade chocolates to the community.
March 17	Saint Patrick	Hold a nature event. Saint Patrick saw the shamrock as a symbol of the Trinity.
March 22	World Water Day (UNESCO)	Show a film about the scarcity of clean water for so many of our brothers and sisters around the world.
March (40 days)	Lent	Present the 5Rs for Lent: reduce, reuse, recycle, repair and revere.
April	Holy Saturday	Emphasize the story of Creation through a play or multimedia presentation.
April 17	Blessed Kateri Tekakwitha	Pray in nature or celebrate a liturgy outdoors.
May 22	International Biodiversity Day (UNESCO)	Be inspired by the protection of biodiversity in the story of Noah's Ark. Organize a talk on this theme.
June 3	Saint Kevin of Ireland	Organize a blessing of animals or a visit to a bird sanctuary, animal shelter or wildlife reserve.
June 5	World Environment Day (UNEP)	Adopt new individual and collective actions to protect the environment. Meet with others to collaborate on a community activity.

Date	Feast or Event	Actions to take
June 8	World Ocean Day (United Nations Environment Programme)	Clean up shores and riverbanks and raise awareness about overfishing.
July 11	Saint Benedict	Saint Benedict lived by the words *ora and labora* – prayer and work. Visit a monastery or a monastery's website to learn more about this twofold approach to life.
September 1	Creation Day (Orthodox calendar)	Pray in nature and reread the Creation stories of Genesis 1 and 2. Celebrate the "Time of Creation" until October 4th.
September 22	International Car-free Day	Set up carpooling and close off parking lots to be used for chalk drawings.
October 4	Saint Francis of Assisi	Sing the Canticle of the Creatures, practise voluntary simplicity or feed the birds or the squirrels.
October (2nd Monday)	Thanksgiving (Canada)	Give thanks to our Heavenly Father for the harvest. Enjoy local bread, wine and produce.
October (3rd week)	Waste Reduction Week (Quebec)	Reduce the amount of goods you consume, and encourage recycling to keep items you are finished with out of landfill sites.
November 23	Saint Clement of Rome	Read Saint Clement's letter to the Corinthians, chapter 20 (God and his Creation).
End of November	Buy Nothing Day	Take up the collective challenge of not buying anything all day.
December	Advent and Christmas	Avoid over-consumption. Share generously with those in need.

APPENDIX III

Sample Environmental Policy

Our covenant with Creation

Grateful to God for the goodness of Creation, and celebrating God's call to us to share with God in the care of our planet, our church covenants to live with respect in Creation. The entire church community is invited to get involved: committed lay faithful and clergy.

Environmental awareness and education are elements in all our programming.

Environmental considerations are an integral part of all our decision making and goal setting.

In committing ourselves to this ministry of ecology, our church has adopted the following specific practices. These practices will be evaluated and updated as needed.

In our WORSHIP, we commit to...

- developing a theology of worship that reflects our call to live with respect in Creation;
- raising awareness of ecological concerns in a theological context.

In our BUILDING, we commit to...

- evaluating our energy consumption and use of fossil fuels in the various sections of our building (church, parish hall, daycare, etc.);
- re-evaluating areas that use a lot of energy with a view to reducing consumption;
- finding ways to reduce the use of fuel;

- exploring new, renewable energy sources (solar, geo-thermal);

- replacing appliances that use a lot of energy with higher-efficiency appliances.

 In our KITCHEN and FOOD CHOICES, we commit to...

- using ecological cleaning products whenever possible;

- taking part in compost pickup programs developed by the municipality;

- serving fair trade coffee and tea.

In our PRODUCT CONSUMPTION, we commit to...

- encouraging all users of our building to use recycling bins;

- using recycled products (made from post-consumer materials);

- meeting with tenants to encourage them to use chemical-free products and use fewer disposable products;

- reducing our use of packaging materials, Styrofoam and plastics, and asking our suppliers, caterers, tenants, etc. to do the same;

- recycling printer cartridges;

- increasing awareness about hazardous waste disposal and promoting municipal eco-programs through our website calendar;

- discouraging the use of bottled water.

In our TRANSPORTATION, we commit to...

- encouraging carpooling programs and the use of alternative forms of transportation in our community;
- encouraging members of the community to consider buying fuel-efficient vehicles;
- encouraging members to make a conscious effort to reduce their carbon footprint;
- emphasizing the benefits of using alternative forms of transport.

PERSONAL NOTES

PERSONAL NOTES

BIBLIOGRAPHY

BENEDICT XVI. (2012). *The Environment*. Huntington, IN: Our Sunday Visitor.

BREDIN, Mark. (2010). *The Ecology of the New Testament: Creation, Re-creation, and the Environment*. Colorado Springs, CO: Biblica Publishing.

BROWN, Edward R. (2006). *Our Father's World: Mobilizing the Church to Care for Creation*. South Hadley, MA: Doorlight Publications.

EPISCOPAL COMMISSION FOR SOCIAL AFFAIRS, Canadian Conference of Catholic Bishops. (2008). *Our Relationship with the Environment: The Need for Conversion*. Ottawa: Concacan Inc.

HAMILTON-POORE, Sam & Jane WAGEMAN. (2008). *Earth Gospel: A Guide to Prayer for God's Creation*. Nashville, TN: Upper Room Books.

IRWIN, Kevin W. & Edmund D. PELLEGRINO. (1994). *Preserving the Creation: Environmental Theology and Ethics*. Washington, DC: Georgetown University Press.

MOLTMANN, Jürgen. (1985). *God in Creation: A New Theology of Creation and the Spirit of God*. San Francisco: Harper & Row.

REEVE, Ted. (2006). *Greening Sacred Spaces*. Toronto: Faith & the Common Good.

SCHARPER, Stephen. (2013). *For Earth's Sake: Toward a Compassionate Ecology*. Toronto: Novalis.

Sleeth, J. Matthew. (2007). *Serve God, Save the Planet: A Christian Call to Action*. Grand Rapids, MI: Zondervan.

Van Dyke, Fred. (1996). *Redeeming Creation: The Biblical Basis for Environmental Stewardship*. Downers Grove, IL: InterVarsity Press.